Ju-Jitsu

THE COMPLETE COURSE

JOHN GOLDMAN

BLACK BELT 6TH DAN

GUINNESS PUBLISHING

Published in Great Britain by Guinness Publishing Ltd, 33 London Road,
Enfield, Middlesex

Jacket design by Stonecastle Graphics Ltd.
Text design and layout by Stonecastle Graphics Ltd.
Front cover illustration by Paul Turner

Typeset in New Century Schoolbook and Helvetica
by Ace Filmsetting Ltd, Frome, Somerset

Printed and bound in Great Britain by The Bath Press, Bath, Avon
"Guinness" is a registered trademark of Guinness Publishing Ltd
A catalogue record for this book is available from the British Library

ISBN 0–85112–754–1

CONTENTS

THE AUTHOR

John Goldman, Black Belt 6th Dan, is a full-time professional teacher of Judo and Ju-Jitsu. In 1980 he constructed one of Britain's first purpose-built training halls (dojos), in Devon, and still teaches there today although he is increasingly in demand by martial arts groups to hold seminars and workshops in many parts of the country.

John has travelled all over the world studying the martial arts including Canada, the United States, Spain, Holland and Japan, where in 1982 he was a guest of the late legendary Budo master, Kenshiro Abbe. On that visit Abbe Sensei awarded John his 4th Dan.

Apart from being a leading authority in the martial arts, John has established himself as a pioneer in methods of personal protection. He teaches and lectures in the West Country where the police regard him as an expert to whom they recommend people for instruction.

John has devised a unique programme of defence-related exercises and these are included in this, his fourth book for Guinness: the others are *Judo; The Complete Course, Self-defence; The Complete Course* and *Taekwondo; The Complete Course*.

Arnold Davies founded the Bushido Zazen International Martial Arts Society in 1969. Actively involved as society sensei and general secretary, he was also recently elected chairman of the newly formed British Budo and Judo Federation, of which he is a founder member.

A PERSONAL WORD
From Arnold Davies 7th Dan

John Goldman is a perfectionist in his field.

I value his co-operation as a guest instructor as much for the warmth and humour which make the carrying out of his sternest instruction a pleasure to young and old on the martial arts mat. This gift of presentation is true, too, of his writing.

I've known John for many years in and out of the dojo and this book is a taste of his rich talent, as will readily be appreciated by all who buy *Ju-Jitsu; The Complete Course.*

Arnold Davies

FOREWORD

With a string of books of the highest standard from Guinness, and foreign translations, John Goldman must be regarded as the foremost writer on the martial arts in Britain today.

The first time I saw John on the mat, in the 1970s, was by chance. I dropped into his YMCA club in my holiday clothes. I was so impressed with John's approach and understanding of the martial arts that I went straight out to buy myself a Judo suit so that I could invite myself to join him on the mat.

He was good then but now, as a 6th Dan, he ranks among the best martial artists I have seen in all my 45 years on the mat. But John is even more than that. He is a populariser who has been responsible for involving hosts of people in different martial arts in his enthusiasm.

He has broken down many barriers between the various arts – his many professional comradeships and friendships are evidenced by the recommendations on the back cover of this book. His ability to put over his atmosphere of warmth and enjoyment in everything he does, comes through in his writing. I know that this book will be a pleasure as well as a means of instruction to all who read it.

Stan Griffiths 7th Dan
President, Universal Budo Association

Stan Griffiths began Ju-Jitsu training while serving in the army in 1947. He now holds the rank of Black Belt 7th Dan and is principal of one of the oldest schools of martial arts in Wales, The Cardiff School of Budo (CSB).
The school, founded in 1949, has played host to many of the world's top exponents of the martial arts. Japanese masters of Judo, Karate and Aikido have visited and taught at CSB but none more famous than the late legendary Judo master Kenshiro Abbe Sensei who became a personal friend to Stan.
In 1982 Abbe Sensei awarded Stan his Black Belt 6th Dan. This was the highest award ever conferred on any person in this country by Abbe Sensei.

NOW AND THEN

Ju-Jitsu is the Japanese name for many of the fighting systems which developed in Japan. Ju-Jitsu is primarily an unarmed form of combat but sometimes weapons are used. There is no standard form of Ju-Jitsu. No one style can be regarded as the authentic or official style. What is common to all Ju-Jitsu systems and styles is that they are combative by nature.

The origin and development of Ju-Jitsu is open to much debate. However, the historians seem to agree that Ju-Jitsu derived from ancient Asian styles of hand-to-hand combat.

The warriors of Japan developed their own methods of throwing, locking and striking. Many of the techniques can only be described as brutal.

They would use their Ju-Jitsu if they found themselves disarmed or partially disarmed on the battlefield. In time more effective fighting skills and defences developed and became formalised and Ju-Jitsu schools were founded.

Ju-Jitsu was often referred to as 'secret techniques' and teachers gave instruction to selected students behind closed doors.

In these special schools new styles emerged. Some concentrated on locks and holds, and the incapacitating of opponents by applying pressure to nerve points on the body. Some schools specialised in throws while others honed their striking skills.

Ju-Jitsu is far from secretive today. Ju-Jitsu means 'flexible science', and this is the key to success for today's practitioner just as it was for the warrior of yesterday.

'Flexible science' somewhat obscures the fact that Ju-Jitsu has a practical application. Ju-Jitsu does not rely on brute strength but upon skill and finesse. It is the use of minimum effort to achieve maximum effect. Applying this principle enables anyone, regardless of physique or stature, to control and release their energy to its greatest potential.

Flexibility also means keeping an open mind. You don't reject this move or that technique simply because it is different. Combine the two kinds of flexibility, of mind and body, and you have Ju-Jitsu, an adventurous, dynamic martial art.

There are many styles of Ju-Jitsu. Some pay more attention to locking techniques, others to striking and throwing. Some schools claim to be traditional in approach, studying the techniques of the ancient battlefield. Other schools practise moves of attack and defence more applicable to modern times and dress. Whatever the approach, there is much overlapping in the practice of techniques. My insistence, in teaching Ju-Jitsu and in practising it, is that everything is workable and practical in any given situation.

The aim of this book is to show the reader the diversity of Ju-Jitsu. No other system in the martial arts uses as great a variety of techniques as do Ju-Jitsu methods. I hope that new participants will be encouraged to join in classes and existing practitioners to develop their skills further.

I have been able in this manual to demonstrate a few techniques. Some you may have seen before, some you may be able to add to your repertoire. But remember, like most jokes, they are not new. They are adaptations of old. And this helps

The Sai and the Jo are just two of the traditional weapons that have come down in the history of the martial arts and are still used in practice. They are unchanged from the original except for the blunted blades of the steel Sai.

to make Ju-Jitsu exciting and open-ended: you are free to develop your own moves at your own pace.

There is something for everyone in Ju-Jitsu. You may practise it for self-defence, as a personal challenge, to acquire a skill, or simply to become fitter.

If you're attracted to it as a popular sport as it is practised worldwide, with team and individual championships, you'll enjoy the chapter on Sports Ju-Jitsu. Weaponry, briefly touched on in this book, is a field of interest for you to explore if you so wish.

Whatever your object, this book should add to your skills, widen your interest in the martial arts and, I believe, open up for you new vistas of enjoyment.

YOUR FIRST STEPS

In a good club there will be an atmosphere of friendliness. If you're not already attending a Ju-Jitsu class, ask at your local library or sports centre for details of clubs in your area. If there are several clubs (dojos) in the area, visit them all. Have a chat with the club instructor (sensei). In any club that has been going for a few years there should be, apart from the instructor, some other high grades practising.

Ability and progress is recognised by the award of coloured belts (grades). The first grade on the way to Black Belt is White. Each club will have a syllabus to work to. This will show the requirements for reaching each grade, the techniques and moves you will need to perform. The syllabus may differ from club to club depending on which Ju-Jitsu organisation the club is affiliated to. There are no laws governing Ju-Jitsu but each association strives to maintain the highest standards.

However, it's not just a question of learning a series of moves on your way to your next belt. There's more to Ju-Jitsu, or any martial art, than knowing the techniques. You will need to demonstrate control, understanding of the rules and codes of conduct and, most importantly, respect for your training partners. The essence of training and development in Ju-Jitsu is co-operation.

This group of happy young people are in the new generation of Ju-Jitsuka. The ages – here 10 to 17 years – mix well and the sexes work together in a natural way.

JU-JITSU – THE MARTIAL LINK

Ju-Jitsu takes on board a host of practical fighting skills. Although of Japanese origin Ju-Jitsu is, in its contemporary form, opportunist.

The Eastern combat arts, some entailing the use of weapons, are termed martial arts. Many have been instrumental in the development of Ju-Jitsu.

Ju-Jitsu has also benefited from the fighting arts that have developed in Europe – the martial arts of the West. The well tried and tested skills such as boxing and wrestling, whose origins can be traced back to ancient combat, have aided the progress of Ju-Jitsu as it is practised today.

Ju-Jitsu is often taught with a traditional approach attributable to the techniques of yesterday's battlefield.

Many Ju-Jitsu schools, traditional and modern in approach, include weaponry as part of training. Just as chess owes its complex moves to the art of warfare, so does Ju-Jitsu derive its weapons, where they are introduced, from the battlefield.

However, many ancient martial arts have now been adapted to allow them to become competitive sports. One of these is the universally popular sport of Judo.

Judo was developed directly from Ju-Jitsu. The Judo player is able to compete, reducing the risk of injury to a minimum by strictly following a code of conduct and the rules of competition. All the strikes and leg locks along with other dangerous moves in Ju-Jitsu have been removed. A contest is won by scoring points. This is achieved by throwing an opponent or holding them down. Victory can also be gained by applying an arm-lock or stranglehold to force a submission. This sounds brutal but rules of application and the watchful eye of the referee ensure that play is kept safe. Many Judo clubs still practise Ju-Jitsu moves. This gives an additional interest to the class and can help to enhance their Judo skills. Ju-Jitsu in Judo clubs often takes the form of Kata. Here pre-arranged sequences of movements and techniques are performed with the co-operation of a partner. It is rehearsed, like acting in a play.

Another popular martial art with its roots in Ju-Jitsu is **Aikido**. This, like Judo, was developed in the last century. Aikido followers can choose either a traditional form or a sporting system. The emphasis in training, whether for sport or art, is based on defence rather than attack. As with Judo the principle behind Aikido is, essentially, non-resistance. When an opponent is off guard, or off balance, then is the time to apply a counter-move and technique. Locks to the wrist and elbow joints along with throws and methods of restraint are all part of training. Weapons, the wooden sword and staff, are used in traditional training practice. In its sporting form an assailant attacks with a knife (a replica), the defender evading the attack and then applying a technique.

Many styles of **Karate** rely on evasion or deflection of an attack too. Then comes the counter-move, usually a punch or kick. This is often followed by tripping or taking the attacker to the ground in readiness for a final strike. Some Karate systems also include weapon training, defending against and disarming an assailant.

If you're already practising a martial art such as Aikido, Taekwondo, Judo or Karate you will see they have a lot in common. Ju-Jitsu is so versatile and diverse in its approach that it can accommodate, with some modification, whatever martial arts skills you already have. You won't find it too difficult to adapt your expertise and acquire a whole new range of skills. With a certain amount of thought and a lot of enthusiasm, Ju-Jitsu promises you a new world of experience and a lifetime of pleasure.

These pictures illustrate the difference (later we learn about the way they blend) between three of the best-known martial arts.

Aikido – Chris stands as passive as a wax model but she is in complete control of her attacker. Any further aggressive move from Steven, however slight, will cost him!

Judo – spectacular, graceful, dynamic. Steven throws Nigel with O Soto Gari (major outer reaping).

Taekwondo and Karate – Ruth keeps her attacker at bay with a piercing side kick. Note her controlled stance, her arms ready for defence or counter-attack.

Ju-Jitsu **THE COMPLETE COURSE**

WHAT'S IN STORE

The number of different techniques that can be applied in Ju-Jitsu practice is countless.

Locks, holds, throws, strikes, chokes, punches, blocks and kicks are all part of Ju-Jitsu – and there's a vast variety of moves in each of these categories.

The Karate and Taekwondo expert will of course be familiar with blocking and striking just as the Judo practitioner will know all about throws and holds.

Imagine combining the Karate moves with the Judo – yes, there's a lot to consider. However, let's first take a brief look at the skills you can use. We'll begin with throws.

Ruth throws Nigel forward over her leg. Note, however, a variant from the conventional grip of the Judo Tai Otoshi (body drop) – Ruth has taken a hold on Nigel's shoulder.

Throughout this book variations of other martial art techniques will be spotted. This is the whole beauty and essence of Ju-Jitsu.

Here Ruth sweeps Nigel's legs from under him, sending him crashing backwards to the mat.

This is one of many ways of blocking and striking out (here with a kick) – see chapter on blocking and parrying.

Here is another combination – punching and striking.

Ju-Jitsu THE COMPLETE COURSE

Ruth applies a lock to Nigel's wrist, at the same time smashing down with an elbow strike.

Locks are versatile. There's no hope for Nigel with both arms tied up whether he's on his feet . . .

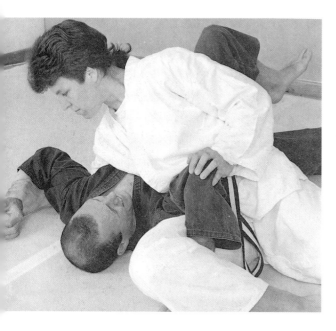

. . . or on his back!

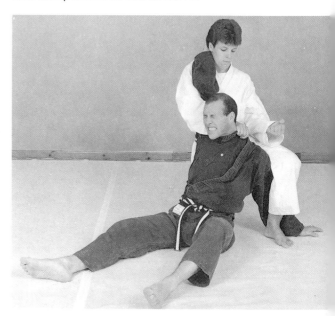

This is a strangle but now Nigel is in a terrible state – one arm locked up, one arm locked down and Ruth still has a hand free to . . . !

YOUR SKILLS – NEW IDEAS

Perhaps you will already be taking part in Judo, Karate, Aikido or Ju-Jitsu classes.

Let's look now at how you, using whatever skills you have, can make good use of techniques from other martial arts.

We'll set up the scene. Your opponent throws a punch. Your training says 'Block and counter-strike'. What's next? Let's find out.

You're a Karateka. Your opponent is about to throw a punch. I'll show you what to do.

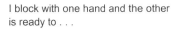

I block with one hand and the other is ready to . . .

. . . counter-strike.

He's still standing! I hit him a second time, in the solar plexus and . . .

follow with . . .

. . . an elbow strike.

Now Judo temporarily takes over – I keep coming forward and step through with my left leg which I now bring round to sweep his leg from under him.

This sends him crashing to the ground.

I am in a good position to stamp down and then . . .   . . . across to make a knifehand strike . . .

. . . quickly followed by a final blow!

You're a Judoka. Nigel threatens to throw a punch.

He lunges forward. I step forward and with my left hand parry his strike. At the same time I have struck out myself.

His position is now weaker. I grip his arm, swing round my body . . .

. . . pulling him over my outstretched leg.

I secure his arm with both hands and drive my knee into his back.

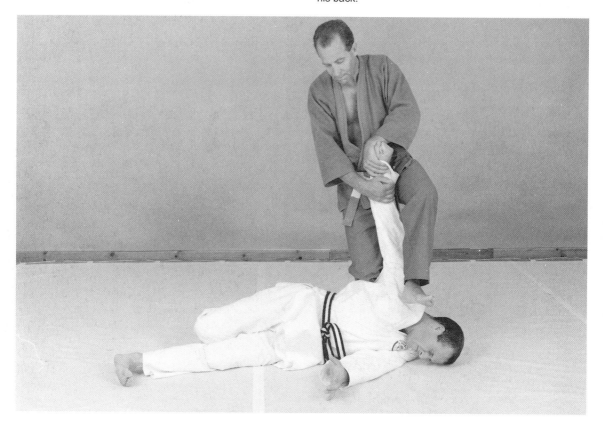

Now I can apply a karate stamp to his head or . . .

. . . bring my heel across his throat.

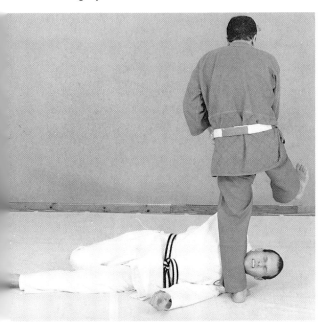

I twist round my body ready to make an axe kick . . .

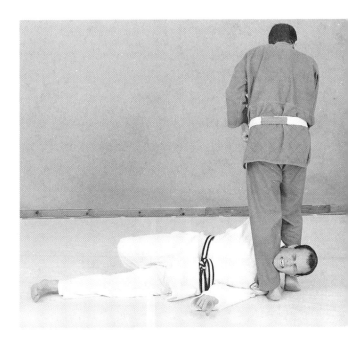

. . . to scissor his neck.

I am in complete control. I twist back to continue with a
Judo technique. I lean backwards and descend . . .

. . . to the mat to apply Juji Gatame (cross armlock).

For the Aikidoist – a karate strike.

Nigel grabs my wrist.

I re-direct his arm to apply a lock that takes him . . .

. . . to his knees. My right leg is ready to . . .

. . . (here's your Karate) strike into his jaw.

I step back and round, bringing him forward. I have control of his arm, giving me a number of options.

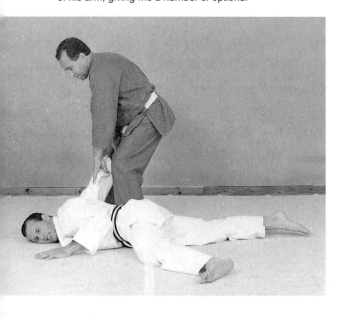

I can either move round and while standing lock his arm, or . . .

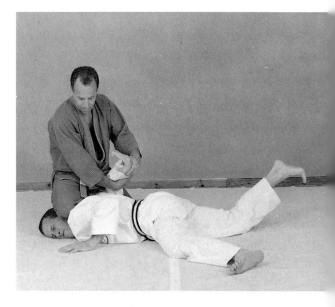

. . . move to a kneeling position to control his head and apply a lock.

TAKING CARE

Safety is number one priority in Ju-Jitsu. The pace may be fast and the training tough but nobody should get hurt. Enjoyment in the dojo is paramount.

So you've decided to give it a go. Begin training in something loose – tracksuit and teeshirt will be fine.

But just before you start, attention to a few personal details. Remove all hard or sharp objects such as watches, rings or hair grips. If your hair is long, tie it back. Training in the dojo is done barefooted on the matted practice area (tatami). Check to make sure your finger and toe nails are kept short. Not only can long nails scratch your partner but they may get torn if caught in your opponent's costume.

In the dojo you conduct yourself in a proper manner at all times. You bow (rei) when you enter the dojo. This demonstrates your desire and commitment to a session of serious practice. Etiquette and discipline are as much a part of training as the learning of techniques. We need teachers and we need partners to practise with. They respect each other; acknowledgement of this is shown in the simple act of bowing to each other.

You'll soon be hooked on Ju-Jitsu and it won't be long before you'll want to be wearing the correct outfit. The best place to buy a Ju-Jitsu uniform (gi) is from your own club. The colour of the gi may differ from one association to another. Some wear an all-white uniform, others white jacket and black trousers. The gi could be red or come with a stripe down the trousers or sleeve. It really doesn't matter. Generally the gis are similar in style, made from cotton, comfortable to wear and easy to clean. It is important to keep your body and costume clean. If the practice is dirty there could be a health hazard. Keep your feet covered until you step onto the tatami.

Bows acknowledge that you and your partner are into study and practice together and respect each other accordingly. But a bow is not just a bow. It can vary from the less pronounced bow at the beginning of practice (below) to the deep ceremonial bow.

Before the session begins there should be a briefing on safe practice and the way in which the session will be conducted. This should ensure good order on the mat.
Uniforms supplied by J Milom Ltd.

Ju-Jitsu is for everybody. Ruth and Karen take time out to model different kinds of uniform (Ju-Jitsugi). You will see them working together later in the book.

SHAPING UP

You don't need to be super-fit to do Ju-Jitsu. However, it won't be long before you're surprised how much fitter you feel taking part in Ju-Jitsu classes. Just one cautionary word: if you have any doubts about your health, consult a doctor before you join a Ju-Jitsu class.

When you start practising you will of course find things a little strange if not strenuous. It would be unusual for anyone, even sports people, not to ache a bit after trying out something new.

Preparation is vital before entering into any physical activity. So go steady. You won't be asked to do anything you can't do and your instructor will have a prepared plan of action for you to follow.

Class will begin with a warming-up session. This period prepares the body for exercise. There are two main aims in warming up. First, to mobilise the joints and second, to raise the pulse rate.

The shoulders, neck, elbows, wrists, hips, knees and ankles all need to be warmed up before any vigorous exercise. This is done with mobility exercises which should be rhythmic and flowing.

These movements will help to increase the flow of synovial fluids to oil the joints. They also help to make the surrounding tissues more pliable. Loosening a joint helps to maintain and increase its range of movement. More important, mobility of the joints will help to prevent injury.

There are many different mobility exercises. Your instructor will demonstrate these. For example: mobilising the shoulders (and this must always be done before loosening up the neck) is achieved simply by resting your fingers on your shoulders and then turning small circles with the elbows. Gradually increase the size of the circles. If this is uncomfortable, make the circles smaller again.

The second aim in warming up is gradually to raise the pulse rate. This will increase the blood flow throughout the body. The cardiovascular system – the heart, lungs and circulatory system –

needs to be prepared. It should be 'ready, willing and able' to safely take on any work demands. Next, for instance, will come your exercises.

But don't exhaust yourself; raise the pulse gradually. Walking on the spot, jogging or skipping are all pulse-raising exercises.

Now that you're warmed up, stretching exercises can be performed (your instructor will decide these).

What I want to tell you about is the exercise *programme*. This may not be what you expected. You may have had in mind sit-ups, press-ups or tuck jumps. These are all fine and could be included. However, the programme I have designed has a specific purpose. I'll explain.

Movements, powerful and well practised, are essential to Ju-Jitsu and self-defence. A keep-fit enthusiast will practise fitness routines every day. Practitioners of Ju-Jitsu should also practise each day. Exercise, yes, but these are different exercises from those of the fitness or aerobic student. All the movements in my programme relate to specific Ju-Jitsu/defence moves.

Look at the line drawings on the following pages and think how you'd use the exercises in a combat situation. Some are designed for striking out, others for evading an attack. Many can be used to release yourself from the grips of an assailant. Throughout the programme I've added real-life pictures of how the exercises can be incorporated into Ju-Jitsu practice.

Each exercise should be repeated eight times before passing on to the next one. Build up a rhythm following on from one set to another. Imagine a target, an attacker; strike out to the left then swing out to the right. Practise these exercises daily, gradually building up the effort you put into the movements.

And enjoy them! They'll help your Ju-Jitsu practice and you'll feel fitter too.

Here we go. These first three are not just stretching exercises. They give that extra flexibility and extension to the arm which increases the power of hand strikes.

The palms are uppermost.
Shrug vigorously.
(Remember, eight times)

1

Now push out.
Extend from the shoulders.

2

Push down.
Extend from the elbows.

3

Thrust the palm forward.
Note the arm is fully extended.

4

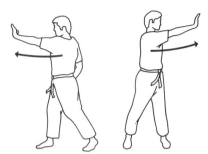

Now thrust across the body.

5

From theory into practice. Nigel grasps Ruth's collar. Ruth at once responds with a palm-heel strike, as in the exercises.

An unwelcome hand (Nigel's) on Ruth's shoulder: she slams in a backfist (as you do in the next exercise, below).

With your fists clenched, pull your arms open and back.

6

Swing

7

Attacked from behind, Ruth swings back both arms, delivering a knifehand blow.

Swing up from a lower position. Then change to the other arm. This and the next exercise use a backfist strike, momentarily moving away from the attacker and then lashing back.

8

a Swing forcefully across the body.

b Then return with a clenched fist and strike.

c And repeat . . .

d . . . on the other side.

9

Grasp your wrist.
Swing back your elbow.

10

You practise different forms of elbow strikes to be ready for anything that may be thrown at you. Here Ruth has parried (see exercise 17) a blow keeping her elbow ready for a strike.

Clench your fist. Pull back the elbow hard. The side view shows the elbow drawn back and knees bent. (This gives extra force.)

11

a Bring the knee across your body and . . .

b . . . thrust your leg out to the side.

12

a Raise the knee and . . .

b . . . snap out your leg.

Note: the knee raise can be used as a separate exercise – remember, eight times with one knee, then change to use the other knee.

13

In this exercise programme kicks are kept low. Here as Nigel approaches, Ruth stops him with a smart front-kick.

Practise this and the following exercise with bold swings. Both these movements will help build up power.

a Start from a relaxed position.

b Swing your arm across . . .

c . . . up and around.

14

a Relax.

b Step forward, arms swinging up from the solar plexus.

c Lower your arms as you . . .

d . . . step back.

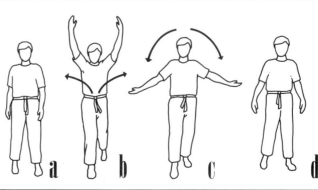

15

Left: Exercise 15 in action. Ruth is fully committed. Both arms are thrust skyward hitting Nigel's chin on the way up. She holds her leg ready to drive her knee upward as in exercise 13.

Above: Now the exercise below. Nigel makes a grab at Ruth. She steps to the side and parries. (Ruth could now, using another exercise, strike out).

The following three exercises are for evading or parrying an attack.

a Relax.

b Step to your right and . . .

c . . . bring your left foot back as you . . .

d . . . pivot on your right foot.

(Note how the arms come into play)

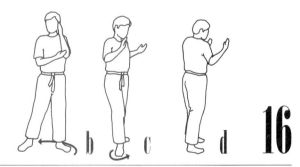

16

a With arms spread . . .

b & c . . . step round (don't forget to come back).

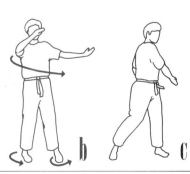

17

a Relax.

b, c & d Step diagonally forward and around. Large circular movements of the arms are vital to this exercise.

18

You may find yourself on the ground.

Here is a cycling movement. Also move your arms in a guarding action. Let's see it in action.

19

There are many things you can do at ground level – how about this snap action? This position also facilitates getting up from the ground as will be demonstrated later.

a Raise hips.

b Now turn, tucking one leg through the gap made by the bent leg and push through . . .

c . . . until the turn is complete.

Left, facing page: As Nigel attempts to get closer, Ruth lashes out, first with one leg then the other.

Ruth's pinned to the ground, but is all lost? Of course not! That is what this last exercise is all about. Ruth has thrust up her hips and is now beginning to turn Nigel off. (She could, as she thrusts up her hips, have made a hand strike to his face – as shown earlier in this exercise programme.)

UP AND DOWN

When you're on the mat, you are on red alert. One minute you're on your feet – the next you're tumbling to the ground. That's Ju-Jitsu!

We've talked about safety, courtesy, discipline, respect and we're warmed up. Now you're ready for the next stage, breakfalling. Ju-Jitsu practice entails throwing and being thrown. Learning to fall correctly is vital to training.

The tatami is specially made to absorb some impact. Even so, it's asking for trouble if you're not well prepared. It doesn't matter how skilled you are, there is always the chance that you'll be caught off balance and find yourself falling to the ground.

Breakfalling is an art in itself. You can be thrown in all directions, to the side, to the back or to the front.

Some organisations hold breakfall competitions. Here flip-over breakfalls, handstand twisting falls and many more are executed in crisp fashion. However, don't get too ambitious at the start. Let's begin with a basic fall – the side breakfall.

The mat is an important part of your equipment. Falling is a partnership between you and the mat. You need to get acquainted. Your instructor will show you exercises to introduce you to the idea of slapping the mat before you actually start falling. When you are ready for real falls you start from a low level.

Nigel is at crouching level for starters.

He swings his right leg across his body. He has now become unbalanced. He therefore prepares for a fall. He quickly looks to the space into which he will fall. His right hand is ready . . .

. . . for the breakfall. He slaps the mat with his arm
outstretched, fingers together. Slapping the arm down in
this way takes the impact of the fall from his body. Note: he
has also turned on his side to lessen the chance of a jolt to
his back.

There must be an immediate recoil from the breakfall – this
entails bringing the hand up as a guard to the face. (This
defence is essential because your attacker may follow
through with a hand strike or kick.) You can't stay like this.
Either you get up – if you're not under further attack – or
you go into a defence position (see exercise programme).

Feeling more ambitious? Now fall from a standing position.

Swing your leg – and . . .

. . . down you go . . .

. . . and breakfall.

Another reason for bringing your hand smartly up to your face after a breakfall: suppose an opponent forces you to turn yourself onto your stomach? Your bent arm now permits you to be rolled over without damage to your shoulder. If your arm had remained outstretched, your arm and body would have been in conflict and something would snap.

It is essential to practise breakfalls after warming up – time will be given to this at the beginning of every class. Your instructor will show you how to make other basic breakfalls to the front and to the rear. I now move on to basic rolls.

Back to ground level to begin. Ruth is kneeling, relaxed, with the toes of her back leg tucked under (this is important).

Helped by her curled toes, Ruth pushes forward to create a circular shape. Study this picture carefully to note the position of her arm and hand. As she makes to propel herself forward, Ruth turns her head towards the rear and . . .

. . . over she goes. The turning of the head and curve of the arm have allowed her body to roll smoothly forward and . . .

. . . over. Note how Ruth has ended in the strong position in which she started – with toes tucked under.

The tucking in of the toes in this stance gives her stability. This is important for dealing in ground grappling or for . . .

. . . getting to your feet and facing your opponent (he could be coming after you). Note how Ruth has, on rising from the kneeling position, pivoted on the balls of her feet to come up into a strong posture – ready for her next move.

ON GUARD

Good posture and control of your body movements are essential. When you are practising techniques with a partner, you are faced with a familiar problem: you are both aware of the formal succession of movements and you are prepared to carry this through in copybook style. If, however, you are too rigid, you are not preparing yourself for competition or combat where surprise, and initiative in dealing with surprise, is the order of the day.

By all means 'go through the motions' with a partner, but be sufficiently relaxed to test each other's skills. It is both more interesting and more productive to maintain an element of challenge during practice or 'friendly' bouts.

Even under pressure, try not to be tense. You need to be relaxed, knees slightly bent. You want to be able to move swiftly and easily from one position to another. You may need to side step, move forward to counter-attack, or retreat. At all times you need to be in a comfortable position, ready for action.

Nigel takes up a fighting stance. Note the body language. Nigel's signal is of aggressive intention; mine is that of a defender – at ease and ready for anything.

From this upright posture (relaxed with knees slightly bent) I can attack or defend. You will soon learn how to distribute your weight to achieve a stance that is comfortable for you. Remember, you need to be able to switch instantly from one move to another – remaining in control at all times.

It is just as important to have good posture on the ground as it is when you are on your feet. You have seen some of the positioning on the ground in the exercise programme, but now let's look at the art of getting up from the ground. You must keep your assailant in view – prepared for what he may do next.

Here is an actual situation:

You are on the ground with your opponent coming at you. You are ready for him. You use the same snap action as in the exercise programme (number 20). You strike out at his knee.

Your opponent is now on the ground and you are in a good position for getting up.

Keeping your eyes fixed on your attacker, you come into a kneeling position. From this you can step back . . .

. . . on to your feet. Now you are ready for your next move.

READY FOR TARGET PRACTICE

Plan, plan, plan. You've got a split second to select your response to an attack!

Blocking, deflecting, striking out – one of these could be your move. You need to know what body-weapons are at your disposal. Do you know where to direct them?

First, know your body. Here are some of the more vulnerable spots.

CAUTION Ju-Jitsu was originally used for self-defence – it was bloody dangerous! You are now practising it as an art or a sport. Take care! For art you stop short of full contact. For sport you are, in addition, padded up.

There are many ways of using your body weapons – hands, feet, elbows etc. Here I discuss some of them.

Practice will make almost instinctive the ability to identify vulnerable points on an opponent's body.

Carlie points out one of the better known targets. I discuss with the class some of the lesser known ones.

The patella (or kneecap) takes its strength in impact from the convergence of many muscles from the upper and lower leg.

This strength is conveyed to the foot. I show how the heel can stamp down and the ball of the foot can be used for kicking out.

The force is now transmitted as a side kick.

Parts of the body such as the elbow, so important in attack, are also vulnerable in a defensive situation as targets. It is essential when they are serving as weapons that they are used with the utmost precision.

Much of the power in your hand is transferred from the shoulder and upper body. In the picture, Ruth has made a knifehand strike. I show her how to follow on with an upset punch aimed at the attacker's solar plexus.

Ruth, with her arm extended, has focused her energies on a palm heel strike. She could have used her fist coiled in such a way that a flat striking surface is formed. Another way would be to make an extended knuckle strike.

YOUR RESPONSIBILITY

One final word before you go into action. Ju-Jitsu, like other martial arts, is based on fighting skills. However, we do not train to 'fight'.

You may have joined a class because you want to gain more self-confidence or learn self-defence skills. It is only in extreme circumstances that any of the moves you learn could be used outside the dojo. They should never be regarded as a 'party piece' or used to fool around with friends.

The law states that you can use reasonable force to defend yourself. You do only what is necessary to stop the attack and get away. It is uncommon for martial arts practitioners to find themselves in a situation where they need to call on their 'fighting' skills. Training in Ju-Jitsu instils a sense of awareness, confidence, and, yes, assertiveness, but these will guide the responsible practitioner away from potential danger rather than into confrontation.

KATAS

You're on the mat, warmed up and ready for action. You've practised some basic punches, kicks and strikes. What next?

First, imagine an opponent approaching – on guard. How is he going to attack? The fact is, you never really know. However, by practising, over and over again, movements for defence and counter-attack, you will sharpen your reflexes – you'll become more prepared for the unexpected.

One method for honing your responses is to practise a variety of movements put together in a sequence, a kind of drill. You move from one technique to another, imagining yourself countering an attack: block, strike, block, block, strike. Keep in good posture: your guard up, hand cocked ready to strike, your leg ready to snap out. These patterns of body movement techniques are called Katas. The Katas may vary from style to style but are essentially the heart of all Ju-Jitsu practice. Some Katas are practised as a solo exercise, others with a partner. A Kata can include strikes, throws or locks, in fact any form of attack or defence. Katas are characteristic of all the martial arts.

Because the movements and techniques of Katas are pre-arranged, practice is safe but nevertheless demanding. You need to know when to attack, when to defend. Practice must be meaningful. You put real effort into the blocks, punches and strikes, at the same time keeping full control. You need to 'feel' the Kata.

My exercise programme illustrated in the earlier chapter is similar to the Kata. Practising the programme each day will help you develop powerful and controlled movements, important to the Katas that you're now going to practise.

This first Kata is a solo exercise that includes blocks, strikes, punches and kicks. Nigel takes you through the sequence step by step. Are you ready?

You begin from a ready position, perform the sequence and end at exactly the same spot where you began. It may be difficult at first but with practice you'll find your way back all right.

Nigel at the ready.

He steps sideways making an elbow strike . . .

. . . and then a downward blocking backfist.

He prepares for . . .

. . . a side kick (he retains his guard).

Now a change in direction. He pivots . . .

. . and steps forward making a palm heel strike.

Stepping forward, Nigel aims a punch.

Now he prepares to turn back (checking quickly on his opponent's intentions).

He swings round with a backfist strike.

Now a reverse punch followed by . . .

. . . a front stamping kick.

In a guarding stance, Nigel prepares for the next move.

He brings his back leg through . . .

. . . to make a front kick.

Preparation (again) to turn and . . .

. . . block.

Stepping forward, Nigel at first makes an upset punch followed by . . .

. . . a further step and straight punch.

As he prepares to turn, with a check on his opponent, he makes a knifehand and . . .

. . . whips round with it on his imaginary opponent.

Nigel now brings his right hand into play. He makes a ridgehand, bringing it round . . .

. . . to strike.

Now one final move. Nigel draws his right leg to his left leg and ends this Kata at the same point at which he started.

I'm not going to overwork Nigel in this Kata. His only function is to take hold of my wrist. But look what happens when he does.

Nigel has a firm grip on my wrist. His role is, from here on, passive but he is in for a painful time. I will now apply locks to his wrist, arm and shoulder. In this Kata I show just some of the possible techniques. Once he attaches himself to me, he's sunk. I don't let him go. I take complete control and manipulate his arm in a variety of ways.

My left hand grips his right hand to keep it where it is. My right hand now comes into play, turning the tables on him.

Now a quick change to a figure four lock. I let go of his hand (he still has hold of my wrist).

I step forward raising my arm: Nigel's arm has to come with me. My left hand slips through to complete the figure four lock.

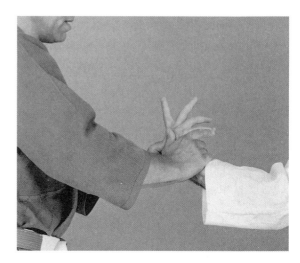

My left hand now takes hold of his right hand, my thumb to the back, my fingers to his flesh palm. I step back, twisting his wrist outwards. My right hand comes into play to give added force.

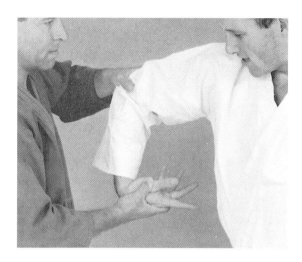

My right hand, from a secondary function, now takes control as I move round to Nigel's right side. I push down on his elbow with my left hand and my right hand pushes upwards – a painful sandwich for Nigel.

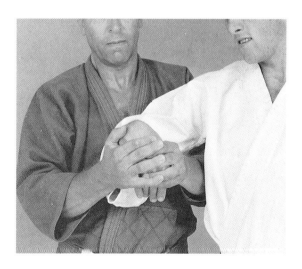

My body enters the fray as a supporting weapon. I jam Nigel's elbow against my lower chest, forcing his wrist and arm back with both hands.

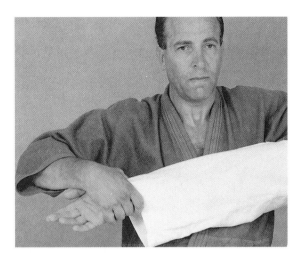

Now a shift to an elbow lock. Holding his outstretched right arm firmly against my body, I pull back his wrist. My left arm meanwhile prevents any body movement from Nigel which would help him escape. The elbow lock is now on.

Another elbow lock, on the way to . . .

. . . my applying this lock to his elbow and wrench to his shoulder.

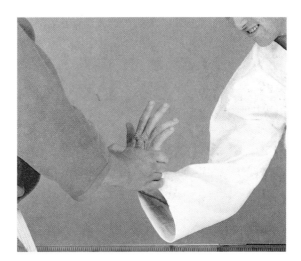

A quick turn brings me in front of Nigel: momentarily I let go with my left hand. Look back to the picture on page 56, bottom right. I apply a similar lock but in this movement I step back, curling his hand over his wrist joint and drawing him down. (This Kata shows only locks, it would be possible to finish Nigel off with a kick.)

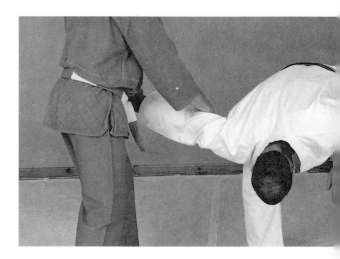

Back to another elbow lock before I step into . . .

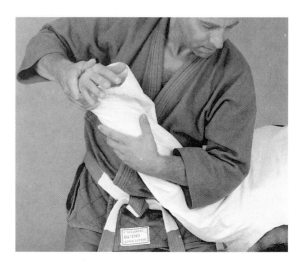

. . . a final wrist-shoulder-elbow lock!

You have been through the Kata. You will see how careful you must be to stop short of causing damage. You will be well aware that final conclusions to the techniques you have seen in this Kata are missing. These can be discussed but only acted out with utmost restraint. Certainly they should only be put into practice by thoroughly experienced Ju-Jitsuka.

Go back two pictures in the Kata. What could happen to Nigel?

I send Nigel crashing to the floor. Taken to its unthinkable conclusion this would end in muscle and ligament damage, or dislocation and fracture to his shoulder and arm.

In the present-day practice of Ju-Jitsu, I need not say, this must never happen.

BLOCKING AND PARRYING

When you are attacked you act swiftly, reverse the tables, and take complete control of the attacker.

In this chapter we learn how to defend and counter-attack. First we learn some basic moves, then polish them.

If you follow my exercise programme and practise the Katas, this will help you develop body movement and co-ordination in readiness for the next stage – blocking and parrying.

Learning to block and parry an oncoming blow is an essential part of Ju-Jitsu training. Blocking is often thought of as a hard smashing of limb against limb, strength against strength. This is true of some styles of Karate. However, it isn't true of Ju-Jitsu – remember, flexible science.

In Ju-Jitsu the blocking actions are made in a way that deflects the force of the attacking limb – the sting is taken out of the attack. This is achieved by a twisting motion with your hand, wrist or forearm as you block. You block using a clenched fist or open hand, ready to catch or trap the attacking limb.

You've avoided, deflected or trapped the oncoming blow. Now you are free for your next move. Your opponent is momentarily off guard since he has failed to hit the target. You could quickly counter-strike. On the other hand you could re-direct the now weakened attacking limb into a vulnerable position – and in you come applying a lock, a wrenching of the joint. Or you could redirect the attack, unbalancing your opponent, executing a throw, tumbling the assailant to the ground. Whatever you decide to do, you must move smartly. Now let's make a start.

There are four ways in which we can make a block: rising upwards, downwards, inwards or outwards. Let's begin practising these four blocks against a punch.

We'll use three punches in this exercise. The first punch is aimed at head height, the second at the chest and the third down towards the stomach/groin region. These three body areas are referred to as high, middle and low.

Begin with your partner making right-handed attacks: high, middle and low punches. You block these with your right hand, deflecting the blow and immediately counter-striking. Further strikes, locks, holds or throws could follow until the attacker is immobilised or weakened to the point where he submits – but we'll come to that later. First the attack, block and counter-strike.

We meet Karen and Ruth again as they square up to each other. The first three sets show right-handed blocks and parries against right-handed attacks – high, middle and low.

Karen throws a punch to Ruth's head. It is blocked by Ruth's rising and twisting forearm. This deflects it rather than meeting it head-on.

Ruth follows with a punch.

This time Karen throws a mid-aimed punch. Ruth steps in and blocks; the turn in her upper body helps to make the parry effective. Her arm is now ready . . .

. . . to whip back and strike.

Ruth steps to the side to parry a low punch and counters
with . . .

. . . a side kick to Karen's knee.

There are many other ways to meet an oncoming blow. You need to be ready to deal with a right or left-handed attack: there are no rules on this. With experience you will have ways at your command to block and counter-strike in one move. We take things step by step.

In the next three sets Karen still aims high, middle and low punches. But this time Ruth will parry with her left hand, counter-strike with her right and – suddenly – throw Karen to the mat. In this section we go only so far: your aim is total and final control over your attacker but for conclusions you will have to wait for the next chapter.

Ruth steps in to parry the attack and . . .

. . . Karen to the ground.

Karen is creased forward under the blow. Ruth now has freedom to . . .

. . . turn in for a throw.

Over she goes.

A low punch from Karen is neatly blocked, upsetting her balance.

Ruth steps in with an elbow strike. Karen's position is so weak that Ruth is able to take complete control.

Following the elbow strike, Ruth wraps her arm around Karen's head. She spins, taking Karen with her. Ruth, turning and pulling, throws Karen over her outstretched leg . . .

. . . to the mat.

The throws you have just seen meet the situations presented. There are many more throws that could have worked. Feel free to use them.

We now move on to blocking and parrying with locks rather than throws. Some of these locks you will have met in the Kata.

Ruth and Nigel face up to each other.

Nigel's punch to Ruth's head is neatly blocked as she also prepares to . . .

. . . grab his wrist. She steps in front of Nigel, her left hand rotating his arm down into . . .

. . . an arm and shoulder lock.

Ruth parries Nigel's punch with her right arm, her knifehand poised to . . .

. . . strike out at his neck. Her left hand controls his punching arm by clasping it against her neck.

From the striking position, she draws first her right hand then her left to his elbow and . . .

. . . steps back, pulling Nigel forward and down into an elbow lock.

Nigel punches low. In parrying the blow, Ruth also prepares for her next move.

She steps forward. She is close to Nigel's body as she raises his arm until it is positioned . . .

. . . ready for her to pull it . . .   . . . over her shoulder.

Ruth meets another low punch by parrying and counter-punching. Nigel's position has been weakened.

Ruth takes his attacking arm with both hands, steps in close to him, ducks under his arm and . . .

. . . turns, keeping a firm grip on his wrist. She rotates his trapped arm over and . . .

. . . down. Note Ruth is applying an arm and shoulder lock just as she did when dealing with an earlier attack by Nigel (page 70). The versatility of Ju-Jitsu allows the same technique to be used in varying situations and by different methods.

DEALING WITH KICKS

You have learned to avoid and deal with a punch. What about a kick?

In Ju-Jitsu you have to be prepared for anything that comes at you: a high kick, a mule kick. As with any defence against a punch, you move quickly into a safe position for your counter-attack. You pay special attention to parrying a kick. The power of an attacking leg can be greater than a punch, you don't want to meet it head on!

Several options are open to you. You could move, parry and counter-strike. Generally, as you parry you are safer moving outside of and away from the kicking leg – you don't want to be caught with a follow-up strike. However, circumstances may not allow this. In a real-life attack, a wall or a vehicle might obstruct you, so you also need to practise moving into the attack. I'll demonstrate various moves against kicks later on in the book but for now here is one example.

Ruth prepares.

Nigel kicks. Ruth scoops up his kicking leg and steps in with a palm heel strike to Nigel's face. This unbalances him. Ruth steps forward again . . .

. . . positioning her right leg behind Nigel's one supporting leg. Ruth continues to push him back, her hand on his chin. Ruth now pulls back her leg to . . .

. . . crash Nigel to the floor. Note Ruth has continued to raise the leg she scooped – this helped Nigel on his way!

COMBINED ACTIONS

Ju-Jitsu is versatile; you are free to develop your own moves at your own pace.

As your expertise increases, you will find yourself ready to respond to a specific attack, say a punch, in several different ways. You may decide to block and counter-punch. You may choose to parry the oncoming blow and then apply an armlock. You may avoid the strike altogether, counter-strike and then throw your opponent to the ground.

In this chapter you will see illustrated a variety of attacks: punches, kicks, strikes and grabs. The techniques demonstrated in response to these attacks are just a handful of a vast store of tried and tested possibilities. Some look simple, others complex.

When you are attacked, the first thing to do is to defend and weaken your opponent. This is achieved by striking out, targeting one of the vulnerable points of his body or, by applying a block or parry, unbalancing him. Now you can move in with your technique.

You may choose to approach some of the moves demonstrated in this book in a slightly different way, taking advantage of your particular build or strengths. Whatever you do, if it works for you, it's right. But remember you need not only to ward off and deal with an attack but take and remain in complete control of the attacker – you don't want them to spring back!

We are now going into a series of defence and counter-moves stemming from three aggressive openings – a punch, a grab and a kick. We'll then look at how to defend from a ground position.

The initial group of actions in this chapter stems from that all-familiar attack – the punch.

This first sequence involves all manner of responses; a parry, a counter-punch, a kick, an elbow strike, a throw, a strangle and a lock.

Nigel, in fighting stance, is preparing to throw a punch.

As Nigel punches, I move in to meet whatever he has in store for me. In fact I do three things at once: I parry his attacking arm, counter-strike with an upset punch, and kick him in the leg. Emphasis: all these moves are simultaneous.

Now another triple action: the foot with which I kicked Nigel moves me forward and takes up a position at Nigel's right side. My left hand (which parried Nigel's attack) takes hold of the attacking arm; the hand I used for my upset punch grabs his collar at the shoulder. I now strike up with my forearm and elbow.

I keep moving forward bringing my right leg behind Nigel ready to sweep his legs . . .

. . . from under him.

Now to finish him off. I follow Nigel to the ground. My right hand still grips his shoulder. By pressing my elbow to the floor I apply a stranglehold. My left hand levers his elbow joint across my knee.

As Nigel squares up for a punch, I plan to deal with him by applying a different kind of backward throw.

I move to the outside and parry his blow with my left hand. My right hand is poised ready to . . .

. . . strike. I keep moving forward bringing my right leg . . .

CAUTION: This stranglehold is applied by putting pressure on the carotid arteries either side of the neck. These life-supporting arteries can, under pressure, cut off the supply of blood and oxygen to the brain. When practising any stranglehold, only go through the motions and only then under the guidance of a qualified instructor.

. . . behind him (left). My hands link to apply a stranglehold.

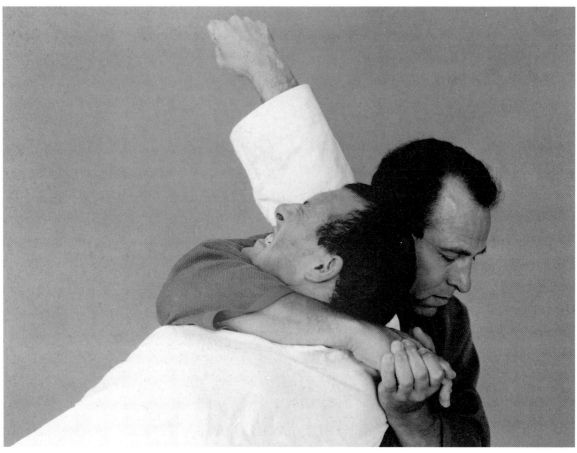

Now to finish it. I shoot my right leg out behind him, at the same time driving him back and down. In this position Nigel is at my mercy: I have no mercy . . .

. . . he goes crashing over my outstretched leg. Note: When you throw over your outstretched leg, take care. Tuck your toes under and keep your leg flexible. This allows you to pivot if you need to; also if your leg is rigid it could be damaged should your opponent fall on it.

Ju-Jitsu THE COMPLETE COURSE

Nigel's next idea . . .

. . . to throw a low punch, finds me ready with a block and a right arm aimed menacingly . . .

. . . as I keep moving forward to meet his forward move. I've spread him out by redirecting his attacking arm, unbalancing him.

I keep the momentum going, stepping forward with my right leg. My right arm lashes into . . .

. . . his throat . . .

. . . catapulting him . . .

. . . to the ground.

Nigel decides . . .

. . . to punch again. I step aside and parry with my left hand, this time pushing his arm towards his body.

My right arm reinforces my left to help . . .

. . . wrap Nigel's arm round his neck. My left hand grips his wrist leaving my right arm ready to strike.

I've tied him up into a neat parcel. I pull on his wrist – his head is wrapped up and in a twist while I administer a final . . .

. . . upward blow . . .

. . . which sends him spinning.

There are other ways of dealing with Nigel's punching attack, apart from throwing.

I parry and counter-strike, first with my fist . . .

. . . then with my knee. My right hand is ready to . . .

. . . grab his jaw. He's still on his feet . . .

. . . as I wrench him upwards into this spine-twisting position. He's as helpless as if I'd thrown him to the ground.

Ju-Jitsu THE COMPLETE COURSE

Nigel is in for more spinal torsion.

I step in and meet his attack with a backfist strike to his temple (a vulnerable point to be targeted with care). My right hand has slipped into position to lock his arm. I move round . . .

. . . behind Nigel, my left hand gripping his jaw to twist his head. In this position his back and spine are under pressure.

I step back, bringing him with me to the ground.

Poor Nigel; what a mess!

Something a little different: a beginning with two endings.

I've blocked with my left and struck out with my right. My left hand grips Nigel's attacking arm. I pivot to my right . . .

. . . and my right hand comes into play, grabbing his wrist alongside my left.

I step in front of Nigel, raising and twisting his arm, enabling me to step underneath in readiness to . . .

. . . drop onto one knee. My body movement has increased the lock on his arm.

He is forced to tumble.

I maintain my grip (the lock's still on) ready for my next move.

I step over his captive arm and . . .

. . . sit down comfortably, trapping Nigel's arm. That's it.

There are so many possibilities in Ju-Jitsu. You could have taken that last sequence to one of a variety of conclusions. For instance, go back to picture four (top left on page 91).

From picture four, instead of dropping onto my knee I have, as aikidoists will recognise, moved in to make Shiho-Nage.

Stepping backwards, I throw him forwards. I bring my left hand into play . . .

. . . as I grip Nigel's hand to lock his arm and take other measures, like stamping on his throat.

Now we deal with an attacker who has made a grab at his victim.

The first two sequences show Nigel taking a hold on my collar. Others show him coming from behind, grabbing my shoulders and then my neck.

The threat.

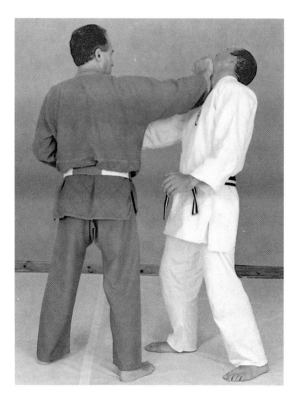

I step forward and strike . . .

. . . reaching round to take hold of Nigel's attacking hand, thumb to the back, fingers to the flesh palm.

I step back, pinning his hand against my chest. My left hand controls his elbow, keeping his arm in position while . . .

. . . a quick wrench, and Nigel's expression tells the story.

Pain brings him to his knees and then . . .

. . . to the ground. I'm not quite finished. I step over his . . .

. . . captive arm . . .

. . . and settle down quietly to wrap first one arm . . .

. . . and then the other.

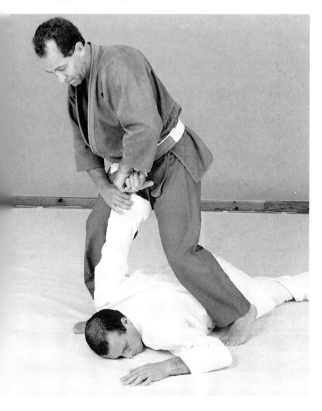

Go back four pictures. Here is another way to tie up both of Nigel's arms. I step across his body and . . .

. . . kneel down.

Now something new. Remember pressure points?

My right hand targets a pressure point. My left hand is ready to bear on targets each side of Nigel's . . .

. . . jaw. This brings him to his toes.

I keep up the pressure as I move to his side, ready to sweep him . . .

. . . to the ground. Note that my right hand, still on his throat, has helped to drive him there. Now to keep him there.

I drive my knee into his chest, taking hold of his wrist and arm (note my right thumb still on the pressure point) to fold them into . . .

. . . this painful lock.

With a slight adjustment I can control him with one hand. My other hand visibly warns him not to make any further aggressive move.

Nigel now comes up behind to grab my shoulder. I am ready to turn the tables. I bring up my left hand to take hold of . . .

. . . his right hand. I have a firm grip on his hand as I duck underneath. My right arm, ridgehand at the ready . . .

. . . lashes into him. I can now step . . .

. . . to Nigel's back. His arm is painfully locked. I am forcing him forward. My right arm pushes down on his shoulder blade, my left arm levers him forward and . . .

. . . to the ground.

Conclusion!

Same beginning (different end).

Above & below: Nigel (with hand twisted) comes to his toes as I step back and under his arm. On the way through I . . .

. . . strike, further weakening him . . .

. . . as I take up a strong position behind him. Nigel's arm is twisted up behind his back. I pull back his head and bend him backwards to crash down . . .

. . . across my knee.

Another attack to twist out of.

I pull down on his arm to relieve the pressure.

I swing my left arm, back fist at the ready . . .

. . . into his groin. Now for a see-saw. I step back and under his arm.

Up I come and down he goes. My hands are linked to put pressure on his shoulder and elbow joints. He's forced forward as I step . . .

. . . out and in front of him. I lever him over my outstretched leg . . .

. . . to the ground . . .

. . . where he will stay.

Note: This arm lock is made totally effective by turning Nigel's head in the opposite direction to the leverage on his arm.

Now wrists take the limelight.

I step forward to Nigel's side and raise my arm high. Nigel's firm grip has done him no good. His wrist is twisted . . .

. . . and his thumb is locked. Before he has a chance to release himself I bring . . .

. . . my elbow smashing down into his chest targeting the breastbone (sternum). He's a weakened man. I could then go on with more strikes or a throw.

Another way of dealing with Nigel's grip on my wrist has the same beginning but a different end.

I step to his side. He's in pain.

I move forward. My hips are in place behind him (left) and I thrust him over them (below).

An interesting question of yours, reader: Why didn't Nigel just let go when he felt his thumb being locked? First, under intense pain it is difficult to think. Second, action must be so quick that the assailant has little opportunity to let go. If he did let go, there are many alternative techniques to apply.

Nigel takes hold again. I have another plan.

By opening my hand and lifting it, almost graciously, Nigel is in the first stage of a painful twist. Before he has the foresight to let go . . .

. . . my right hand comes into play to get his wrist and arm into a twist.

A quick turn of my hands and his whole body is in a twist.

He hits the floor. Now to turn him over . . .

. . . for a complete submission.

Now for kicks. In the next three sequences you see how to move inside or outside of an attacker's leg.

Nigel's posture signals an on-coming kick.

I move to the outside of this attack and scoop up his leg. My scoop is part of a circular movement that will . . .

. . . propel him . . .

. . . back . . .

. . . to where he belongs!

Ju-Jitsu THE COMPLETE COURSE

Nigel switches to his right leg.

I move in, scooping his leg with my left hand while striking out with my right. Now to tip him over.

Note: this shot is taken from the rear to show how I start the tipping job. The arm I scoop with is raised, lifting his leg higher, unbalancing him further.

My right hand bears him down. Note he is now airborne, on the way . . .

. . . over and down . . .

. . . and grounded. I follow up with an axe kick.

What's coming?

It's another kick, another scoop – accompanied by a palm-heel strike.

I reach over to wrench Nigel's leg . . .

. . . forcing him forward . . .

. . . face down to the ground.

Keeping a firm hold of his leg, I prepare to put on a leglock. I step over his captive leg and . . .

. . . kneel down. His leg is now folded, his calf muscles under intense strain.

Imagine yourself on the ground. (In an earlier chapter, On Guard, we showed how to get up. The next sequences show how you can deal with an attacker).

Nigel closes in. I turn on my side, my left foot hooking his right. Note: I remain on guard all the time. I swing my right leg forward to . . .

. . . slam it into the back of his knee. As he falls forward I roll over and come . . .

... to a kneeling position. I am now in a position to apply the same leglock ...

... as in the previous sequence.

Another way. I'm on my bike as in the exercise programme.

I turn to my side, hooking with my right leg and preparing with my left leg to strike his knee. Another action from the exercise programme (**exercise 20**) does the job. I pull back with my right leg and snap out with my left. We are back on the see-saw.

As Nigel goes down . . .

. . . I come up (with his help!) – Wham!

SPORTS JU-JITSU

Developing Ju-Jitsu skills can be a life-long quest. In this book I have been able only briefly to describe Ju-Jitsu training and demonstrate merely a handful of techniques.

Once hooked on Ju-Jitsu you can specialise in one particular area of training. You may develop the skills of joint-locking or learn, with precision, how to attack the nerve pressure points of a would-be attacker.

Whatever you do in Ju-Jitsu it is exciting, challenging and rewarding. It's up to you to decide on your goal and proceed at your own pace.

In this final chapter I want to tell you about one exciting area of Ju-Jitsu that is attracting thousands of people and may be just what you are looking for – Sports Ju-Jitsu.

Many of today's Ju-Jitsu enthusiasts come from a sporting background. Some have competed as Judo players, others in Aikido and Karate.

There are several different ways of planning Sports Ju-Jitsu competitions. Whatever system is used, they are all designed to give participants, whatever their special skills, an equal opportunity.

A popular form of competition entails three two-minute bouts. The competitors are required to demonstrate different skills in each round.

The contestants fight in weight groups, men and women competing separately. A referee controls them and judges keep score.

Round 1 is the random attack round. The two fighters stand apart in the matted contest area, their backs towards each other. Each is allocated an attacker. The two attackers are briefed by the referee: they read a card specifying the kind of attack they must make. Their assaults are launched without hesitation; the attacker must not signal his intentions. They must be all-out attacks, putting the defender fully to the test.

The attacks may vary from strikes to kicks. Even a knife (a replica) may be included. The competitors (the defenders), first one and then the other, respond to the attacks. The one who makes the most practical and realistic defences wins the round.

Round 2 The contestants face each other. They are padded up – head guard, foot and hand protectors and groin guard – at the ready. The action now is free fighting. Punches, kicks, throws, locks and strangles are all in. However, there are rules. The going is tough but no one should get hurt.

Round 3 Here we come to ground fighting. The opponents face each other kneeling. They attempt to gain a submission. This can be done by applying a lock to the arm or wrist. Some leg locks are also permitted. A submission may come from a stranglehold or by attacking a pressure point.

A random attack bout is due to start.

Leigh and John at the back are taking instructions on the kind of attack they will make on Chris and Nigel who, out of earshot, wait to be put to the test.

It's all action in free-fighting. Fully togged up, Chris (left) parries Nigel's kick and is in position to make a counter-attack.

thrown him there!

Sports Ju-Jitsu is certainly not out of reach for the young. Nine-year-old Martin is by no means the smallest boy or girl to find Ju-Jitsu the ideal sport.
Equipment supplied by Ricochet Martial Arts Ltd.

HAPPY DAYS, JU-JITSUKA

Now you know something about Ju-Jitsu and the unique kind of enjoyment you can get from it. For those who have mastered some of its techniques and its spirit, there is a lifetime of fulfilment with endless prospects of new and exciting discoveries.

I hope this book has given you enough to encourage you to embark on that most adventurous of the martial arts – Ju-Jitsu.

Ju-Jitsu is the fastest growing of the martial arts in this country and probably worldwide. It is expanding so rapidly that masses of organisations are being established, each with its own merits, but widely varying in the emphasis on specialist techniques.

Whatever you do, do it in good spirit; take care, enjoy it and good luck.

ACKNOWLEDGEMENTS

My wide extended family in the martial arts know my wife Chris as a social link, always supportive and quietly enthusiastic. She became hooked on Judo in the 1960s. Chris has been my model in previous books and figures briefly in this one.

Another model is my daughter Ruth, a black belt 3rd Dan and herself a professional teacher of Judo and self-defence.

Nigel Hoskins (3rd Dan), almost a son, suffers at the hands of myself and Ruth throughout the book, showing signs of anguish which I hope are not all genuine.

My thanks to all the younger models, too, and to my senior students Karen, Steven, another Chris and Leigh. Also my deep appreciation of his teaching, help and encouragement, on and off the mat, to my friend Stan Griffiths.

Finally: My mother Mabel, as always, clears the table for action and at intervals fills it with grub, making it possible for me to work with my father, Harold, himself a journalist, who edits as we go along.

John Goldman

USEFUL ADDRESSES

Amateur Martial Associations
120, Cromer St
London
WC1H 8BS

Tel: 071 837 4406

British Taekwondo Council
c/o Redfield Leisure Centre
163A, Church Road
Redfield
Bristol
BS5 9LA

Tel: 0272 551046

Bushido Zazen International Society GB
20, Halstatt Road
Millhill
Deal
Kent
CT14 9ED

Tel: 0304 366750

Cardiff School of Budo
Fairoak Hall
Fairoak Road
Cardiff
CF2 4PX

Tel: 0222 224455

Independent Budo Federation, Europe
c/o Antwerpsestraatweg 460
4625 AH Bergen op Zoom
Holland

Tel: 01640 65119

Ju-Jitsu International
73c, Church St
Stoke Newington
London N16

Tel: 081 363 7543

J Milom Ltd
Judo & Martial Arts Equipment
Springfield Mills
Sherborne St
Manchester
M3 8AH

Tel: 061 832 6155

Ricochet Martial Arts Ltd
Meynek House
Station Road
St Columb Major
Cornwall
TR9 6RY

Tel: 0637 881010

Sports Council
16, Upper Woburn Place
London
WC1H 0QP

Tel: 071 388 1277

Universal Budo Association
21, St Johns Road
Exmouth
Devon
EX8 4BY

Tel: 0395 265532

World Kobudo Federation
Canadian Section
259, St Anne Street
Vanier
Ontario
Canada
KIL 7C3

Tel: 613 746 5402